FOR THE SENDER

← music

words →

FOR THE SENDER

Four Letters. Twelve Songs. One Story.

ALEX WOODARD

HAY HOUSE, INC.

Carlsbad, California • New York City

London • Sydney • Johannesburg

Vancouver • Hong Kong • New Delhi

Published and distributed in the United States by: Hay House, Inc.: www.hayhouse .com® • *Published and distributed in Australia by:* Hay House Australia Pty. Ltd.: www .hayhouse.com.au • *Published and distributed in the United Kingdom by:* Hay House UK, Ltd.: www.hayhouse.co.uk • *Published and distributed in the Republic of South Africa by:* Hay House SA (Pty), Ltd.: www.hayhouse.co.za • *Distributed in Canada by:* Raincoast: www.raincoast.com • *Published in India by:* Hay House Publishers India: www.hayhouse.co.in

Book design: Nena Anderson • *Photo Contributors:* Alex Woodard, Nena Anderson, Alden DeSoto, Kim Goodeve, Emily Jackson, Steve Bessant, and Maeve McGoldrick

Previously published in the United States by Alex Woodard: ISBN 9780983988601, LCCN 2011937958.

Library of Congress Control Number: 2012938903

Hardcover ISBN: 978-1-4019-4121-5
Digital ISBN: 978-1-4019-4122-2

15 14 13 12   4 3 2 1
1st Hay House edition, September 2012

Printed in the United States of America

SUSTAINABLE
FORESTRY
INITIATIVE
Certified Chain of Custody
Promoting Sustainable Forestry
www.sfiprogram.org
SFI-01268

SFI label applies to the text stock

Contents

I.   DA CAPO   1

II.   THE LETTER   7

III.   THE AUTUMN   21

IV.   THE SHELTER   39

V.   THE SEARCH   61

VI.   THE WELL   81

VII.   THE BOX   101

VIII.   CODA   111

About the Author   127

DA CAPO *(music)*

to play from the beginning — It., da: from, capo: head.

"Well, bro, maybe you should," Shawn said, the words coming out slow and full of Southern melody. He went back to staring out the window as the mist floated by under the nearly spring, steel-gray sky. I drove. And thought.

I was navigating a rental car through upstate New York, and Shawn Mullins, a singer-songwriter like me, was in the passenger seat. We were on our way to play a show in Mahopac, and I was trying to keep us between the lines on the wet Taconic State Parkway.

He meant that I should write this little book you're holding in your hands. It's the true story of how writing a song about a letter changed my life, but it's also the story of something bigger, because over the course of a year I received three more letters: one from the widow of a police officer killed in the line of duty, one from the director of a homeless shelter for kids, and one from a medic in Haiti. This book is about their stories, too, told through their letters and in songs from a close-knit group of musicians and songwriters.

I'd been telling Shawn how I could feel my life begin to shift as we wrote and recorded songs about those four letters. I was giving myself over to helping other people's voices sing other people's stories, and it wasn't really about me anymore.

He asked if I'd been documenting the process as it unfolded, and I told him I'd written some thoughts down on scraps of paper scattered around my home studio. And, just as I'd traced the route from New York City to Mahopac on the map in the car console, I'd recently drawn lines of connection between those scraps of paper, the four letters, and the journal of life moments I kept on the backs of envelopes, napkins, and hotel-room notepads.

I'd find those life moments, usually written in the present tense, in my backpack after a tour or under the seat of my truck when I was cleaning it out. I'd save the notes in my dresser drawer, but no one ever read them. Those words were written more for me, my own secret record of scenes from my life, tucked away like the unsent letter I kept in a box high on a shelf in my living room.

As we passed the city-limits sign for Mahopac, Shawn smiled and suggested that maybe it's time somebody read those scraps of paper, even if it meant telling my own story as I was letting go of myself. I said I'd thought about pulling something together, some kind of collection of letters, songs, and stories that could somehow benefit a cause we all felt good about.

"Well, bro, maybe you should."

I drove. And thought. And the mist floated by under the nearly spring, steel-gray sky.

When I let go of what I am, I become what I might be.

— Lao-tzu

THE LETTER

Dear Alex:

I wanted to share
with you. I am not a w
know how to articulate
I know how deep.

Me and the leaves are barely hanging on when I get the letter. Autumn is painting change everywhere, and I am turning over a season of my own, although the trees are doing a better job of letting go than I am. Leaves and dreams alike are either dying on the limb or already gone. And so is she.

I am younger, barely out of college, and working a monotonous, entry-level job at a financial-services firm in Boston when I begin to dream with eyes wide open. I stare at my computer screen and dream in flashes and moments, where I see pictures of living an unordinary life somewhere far away from the fluorescent lights and prefab felt walls of my cubicle. Somewhere with a big sky, mountains, and a dog.

A dog would be a real friend, I tell myself. *A dog would fill the space.*

Sometimes I dream about music. I've only begun stumbling through songwriting, but just the thought of someday making a moment in someone's life better with one of my songs makes me feel more alive than anything at my job ever could. *Someday* is a word full of hope, but it's also an escape from the present, and I close my eyes on the crowded subway every morning and dream about *someday.* After work I run along the near-frozen Charles River in my ski clothes imagining a dog at my side, and I spend my evenings and weekends alone, teaching myself to play guitar and writing lyrics in a notebook I buy from a pharmacy down the street.

Maybe *someday.*

I wake up one morning in my tiny loft apartment in
Kenmore Square to Bruce Springsteen singing "Trapped"
from my clock radio. My eyes open to his gravelly voice
promising that someday I will see beyond these walls and walk
out of here. And, in the middle of the Clarence Clemons sax
solo, as I stare into the harsh half-light filtering through the
exhaust-caked windows fronting Brookline Avenue, I get it.

Life is somewhere else.

Later that day I tell my boss that my dreams are waiting out West, somewhere with trees and a dog. I give notice,
and two weeks later I'm reading the goodbye card signed
by everyone in my department, eating goodbye cake, and
drinking goodbye coffee. My older co-workers talk to me in
remember-when tones about chasing their own dreams and
wistfully wave as I turn to face them from the elevator, push *L,*
and wave back as the doors close. The elevator opens into the
lobby, and I walk out onto Federal Street and into a world of
promise.

Over the weekend I pack up my truck, and within two days
I'm pulling off I-80 in Utah, where a box of puppies is waiting behind my aunt's garage door. There are two puppies left
unclaimed, and I throw a knotted-up sock across the floor to see
which one retrieves it first. A tiny black Labrador with soft eyes
stumbles to the sock, picks it up, and makes her way back to me
through the gauntlet of paint cans and cardboard boxes.

She falls over herself and into my lap, and I am in love.
I call her Kona, after the black-sand beaches on Hawaii's
Kona coast. I had written that name down on a scrap of paper
the winter before and pinned it to the wall in my cubicle,
back when I had first started imagining a dog and a life less
ordinary somewhere in the trees.

I find the dog in Utah and the trees in the Pacific
Northwest, where I get a temp job working for an Internet-
software company in Seattle's Pioneer Square. One day I see
a guy with long dreadlocks in the hallway, and he introduces
himself as a bass player who works in the company's tech
department. We talk about music, and he comes over a few
nights later to play some of my songs in the basement. Within
a few months, we have our first show at the University Sports
Bar in Seattle, where I sing until my throat is raw and play
my guitar without a pick until my fingers bleed at the cuticles.
I pretend like I've done it a million times, but really have no
idea what I'm doing.

It's a good start, but that's all it is. I sink into my second-
hand couch every night and earnestly write songs that mostly
speak to loneliness and missed connections, with a hopeful
message that someday will be better than today. I sit at my
kitchen table dutifully addressing postcards announcing gigs
to my hard-earned mailing list, but play to only a handful of
people. I book studio time and write checks to local engineers
to record my songs, only to sell a few CDs.

These cold realities of the music business slowly begin to creep under my skin, and some nights, as I lay alone in bed, I weave a make-believe coat of dreams as protection to keep me warm: dreams of "making it," dreams of having somebody to grow old with, dreams of little feet on hardwood floors. That imaginary coat of protection keeps the cold out, but it also keeps most of myself hidden from anybody else.

My days become some sort of solo waltz, where I bring my left foot up and step to the right, bring my right foot back and step to the left, always moving but hardly ever forward. Barely-break-even touring is bookended by stalled personal and professional relationships, and I find that sometimes chasing dreams is just that: a chase. I tell myself that maybe this crap gig will lead to a better opportunity, and that opportunity will lead to a better gig, and so on, until driving home from a show one night I realize that I've spent most of my 20s trying to be anywhere other than where I am. I remember listening to "Trapped" on the clock radio back in Boston and telling myself, *Life is somewhere else.* But somewhere else doesn't feel right anymore.

And maybe it's because I'm not confident enough yet, maybe I'm afraid to talk to that girl at the bar, maybe I'm a late bloomer. Or maybe it's because I'm burrowed behind that make-believe coat. Whatever it is, I'm alone most of the time, and I cling to the cliché that still waters run deep as an excuse for keeping to myself.

I maintain this constant migration toward solitude while I live in Seattle, avoiding parties and bars unless I'm performing at them. I tell myself that being alone helps me write and connect to people through my songs, although I'm not really sure anybody's listening. So I write because I'm alone, but I'm alone because I write. And while I might write to connect to people, I also write selfishly. I write for me, because writing gives me someplace to put my love. My hope. My fear.

I write about the mystery. I invite it in like an old friend who knows me, and we have conversations about what's going to happen to me. The mystery knows what my wife is going to look like. And where my kids will take their first steps. And if anything I write is going to matter. The mystery knows, but I don't.

One night on the road, after a particularly empty gig in Chicago, I'm far away from anything or anyone familiar and standing in the unforgiving bathroom lights of my hotel room when I see it for the first time. I lean over the sink, closer to the mirror to make sure I'm seeing what I think I'm seeing. My eyes are tired with small wrinkles at their seams, and it looks like a few gray hairs are coming in above my right temple. *I am older.* I stare at myself for a couple of minutes, and after a while it's as if I'm staring at someone else. I turn the lights off and make my way to bed, only to search the ceiling for answers to the questions reflected in the bathroom mirror.

How did I get here?
Do I give up?
Then what?
Alone?

I remember my dad telling me, "Don't be an old man in a young man's game," but that's not the answer I'm looking for. The ceiling holds nothing else for me, and I watch the dancing shadows cast by the blue light of the television until sometime around daylight I finally fall into a broken sleep. I dream of myself as a child on a cold, rocky beach with a gray sky threatening overhead. The child has just come out of the water to find that someone has stolen his clothes, so he stands there holding his privates and shivering. Just shivering.

Shivering, that is, until I fly back to Seattle the next morning and pull into my driveway later that night. Kona's gentle eyes shine like fireflies as my headlights trace across the window, and I can hear her deep bark signaling my arrival. I open the front door, and her tail is wagging so hard that it hits the coat-closet door and bleeds a little, leaving small red brush strokes across the entryway wall. Kona doesn't care, and neither do I. I'm home.

The next morning I paint over the streaks, but it's a futile effort since it happens whenever I leave her and come home; we're both used to her being my constant companion and the unconditional keeper of my heart. I tell her what I'm scared of and share my little victories with her. She listens without judgment, always with love, and ends most of our conversations with a thump of her tail and a search for something to play with to help me refocus on the important things. Being present. Living. Playing.

I take her everywhere with me that doesn't involve an airplane. I sneak her backstage at the small, dirty clubs I'm playing and out of hotels the next morning. One New Year's Eve I'm playing a show in Santa Barbara and come back to the hotel to see Kona asleep behind the front desk, at the feet of the Asian-American hotel manager who points to the No Pets sign on the wall. He says in broken English that she was barking, so he pulled her from the room, but she was so friendly that he couldn't call animal control. That's the first time I realize that she has more friends than I do, just by being herself. She teaches me many lessons like this as time passes, lessons mostly in patience, selflessness, and love.

Long after I get home from Chicago, the scenes from my shivering dream continue to flash through my head. Something has to change, and I wonder if maybe it's my surroundings, so I rent my house in Seattle to a mutual friend to cover my bills and move back to Southern California to be closer to the ocean and my family. I find a little house north of San Diego where I spend early mornings rediscovering my love for surfing and the rest of the day knocking on music-industry doors via phone and email.

Some nights I play shows at local coffee shops and bars, but most nights I run with Kona on the beach before making dinner for myself. I rinse my plate, turn off the kitchen light, and head to the couch, where I write and rewrite songs until Kona's soft steps on the hardwood floor follow me to bed. I lay with fading faith that maybe this next song will be "the one" and someday this will all make sense.

I still carry *someday* with me everywhere, but now I hang on to it like a tree hangs on to its last leaf in the early winter wind, sensing that with one strong gust that leaf will fall. And soon enough it does.

Christmases come and go and come again, and I am disconnected, ground down by the chase, and sitting in the cold white lights of a veterinarian's office when I hear a faraway voice saying that Kona's bones are starting to disintegrate from cancer and that she probably has a week to ten days to live. I don't want to get in a car wreck on the way home, so I hold back, hold back, hold back until I carry her through the front door and lay her down in the living room. I don't stop crying until I fall asleep on the floor next to her.

Even then, I don't really stop.

When I wake up a few hours later, I lift her over the mess of cables and cheap recording gear littering the room and onto my bed. I sit next to her and stare at our reflection in the window until I'm looking through the glass and down into a well carved deep with memories, with only the edge of a dream peeking out from the brackish water that laps against the side. In the well water I see the past 14 years rushing by like a movie in fast-forward.

The scenes fly by fast, from a puppy picking up a knotted sock in my aunt's garage, through those cold, wet nights playing guitar while she slept at my feet, when I wasn't really alone because she was with me. I see almost every moment up to right now, when my eyes come back into focus on the window and settle on our picture framed in the glass.

I quietly shudder and Kona looks up at me and wags her tail once, which she often does at the close of our conversations. It's how she says *It's okay, Dad.* I put my hand on her shoulder. *It's not okay, Kona. Not at all.*

That week I invite anyone who ever knew Kona to a Christmas gathering at my house to say goodbye to her. My new neighbors and some old acquaintances show up, and her vet brings a soft blanket for Kona to lie on. The cancer hurts the worst where it started in her shoulder, so she lays on her less painful side at the top of the stairs where she can see everyone. She thwacks her tail on the hardwood floor as people with wet eyes line up single-file and bend down on their way out to rub her belly, some giving up the fight and crying for what seems like forever with their heads on her disintegrating shoulder.

The last guests make their way down the stairs, past the lit-up tree, and out into the night, where their worlds keep on turning toward Christmas Day, New Year's Eve, and the rest of their lives. I lean against the counter and feel my world sputter a little and lurch forward and back until I pick Kona up, lay her in my bed, sit on the edge, and wait for it all to stop.

She slowly deteriorates but surprises everyone with her bright eyes and resilience, and it is midsummer of the following year before she dies in my living room with her head on my lap. A single tear emerges from the corner of her eye, trickles down her gray muzzle, and disappears into the fabric of my shorts. A friend who is there to help says that it might look like she is crying but it's just her body reacting to death, and I say to myself, *It's the same thing.* I leave the three folded pages I have written to her earlier that day next to her body and cry my way through our old beach run until I can't see through the tears and sit on the sand with my head in my hands, watching everything I thought would happen by now trickle through my fingers into a pool at my feet.

So, me and the leaves are barely hanging on when I get the letter.

Dear Alex,

Every year around this time, I feel a little nostalgic and sad, because this is the season when I lost someone who meant a great deal to me. You see, I am one of the lucky ones, I have

Fall is nature's grace time;
giving you a chance to put things in order, for the dying.
It is a time for remembering.

— The Education of Little Tree

experienced the amazing connection of love with a soul mate. A real kindred spirit. Unfortunately, he passed away a few years ago, but I still consider myself lucky, not only because I have felt true love, but I have lost it as well and that too can be considered a gift; for I now know even more than before just how precious life and love are. Of course, I am not always able to smile through the day, sometimes I still miss him, painfully so. Like in autumn, not only the time of year when he was taken from me, but also the time we loved best. So, every year around this time, when the memories fill me, I write him a letter. I thought I'd share it with you, not so you'd write a song for he and I, but because I think your songs are gifts. Pieces of yourself used to help other people with their stories. So, here is a piece of myself. It is all I have to share in return for the wonderful thing you are doing with your music and your talent.

*   - Emily*

I don't know Emily or how she has heard any of my songs, but folded behind her letter to me is the one she has written to her partner earlier that autumn. I open the parchment-thin pages, and the auburn-colored leaves included in the envelope fall out onto the table along with a photograph of a man with his arms outstretched, who I assume is Emily's soul mate. And the air catches in my throat as I begin to read.

THE AUTUMN

Dear Alex:

I wanted to share
with you. I am not a w
with how to articulate
I know how to say best.

...face as we cudd...

...time where the soul...

I hope it is autumn where...

think of me sometimes when...

the trees and the Jack-o-lante...

I miss you.

Forever ... Your Em

Dear Anno,

The leaves have begun to change again. It began a few weeks ago, but with a subtlety I am not sure I can describe. As if Nature was planning a surprise party, for weeks the plans go on behind your back, bit by bit. Then suddenly one morning you walk outside, and the brisk autumn air screams "SUR-PRISE!" You look up and see all the colors, like old friends: orange, umber, yellow, sienna, burgundy, green, and brown. The trees are ablaze in a patchwork of fiery brilliance that comforts your very soul.

My favorite coffee shop has pumpkin coffee now. I drink it down in gulps that fill my thoughts with memories of autumns past when we carved funny faces in pumpkins and ate caramels as we walked in the woods looking for pinecones. We were so young then, so happy and free spirited. I still feel that way sometimes. It's like a cosmic gift from the universe. It doesn't happen often, but when it does- Oh, the feeling! Like an orgasm for the soul when you feel alive and free of worry. When doubt and fear are strangers to you and you remember what fun feels like. Do you remember fun? We used to have lots of it this time of year; jumping in leaf piles and laughing, hot apple cider flowing in our veins, the smell of cinnamon and spice in the air.

It lasted only a short time before the season of hot cocoa and snowflakes would quickly drift in and frost over our little world, but while it lasted, autumn was a happy time. We were young and in love, and the world was beautiful.

*I still miss you, you know, when the trees are on fire, my
heart yearns for you. When the night becomes chilled and the
hot apple cider is sipped around the bonfires, I still think of you.
Sometimes, I swear I can feel your arms wrap around me at
night when I stand out in the cold. The cool night wind tickles
my neck like the scruff of your unshaved face as we cuddled close
to the fire.*

*I don't know where the soul goes when a person dies, but I
hope it is autumn where you are, too, and that you think of me
sometimes when the leaves blow off the trees and the jack-o-
lanterns are smiling. I miss you.*

Forever . . . Your Em

I can feel my heart beat faster as I crawl inside Emily's
letters and feel her loss and love and gratitude, different from
my own but the same at its source. As I read I realize that I'm
allowed into her words because she received me somehow: she
heard a song of mine somewhere, connected to it, and let me
in. *Someone was listening.*

I show her letters to Sean Watkins, who I've come to know
through the "family dinners" in my neighborhood. The "family" is made up of both neighbors and a diverse cast of local
songwriters and musicians, held together mostly by this

small stretch of San Diego coastline. The dinners are potluck affairs that almost always end with guitars and a mess of other instruments blanketing the floor and furniture. I'm invited to my first family dinner at a neighbor's house that autumn, a couple of weeks before Emily's letters show up.

I walk across the street with my guitar and a bottle of six-dollar wine, stepping through the front door and into a conversation between Jon Foreman and Jordan Pundik, who front the rock bands Switchfoot and New Found Glory. Sean and his sister Sara Watkins, from bluegrass band Nickel Creek, are sitting at the dinner table already, and I recognize a few other people from the neighborhood scattered around the room. By the time the night is over, we've laughed, told stories, played songs, and butchered a cover of Bon Jovi's "Wanted Dead or Alive." I come back home and fall into bed with a small smile and the seed of a feeling like I might belong here.

Autumn takes hold, and my friendship with Sean continues to grow out of that first family dinner. He soon claims his own spot in the corner of my couch and, with one hand on the TV remote and one on his guitar, watches shows about ghost hunting that he never quite believes but still can't stop watching. I show him Emily's letters, and we decide to write a song together because her words resonate with him, too.

Sometimes I write songs for people who tell me their stories, but never with someone else like this, especially in my "leave me alone, I have to write" state of mind. I loosen the reins on that control the afternoon Sean comes over to the house and plays guitar while we hum melodies back and forth. We trade lyric ideas, and I notice how he picks up on different parts of her letter, as if he sees her sentences through another lens.

Sean goes home and comes back a few days later with "For the Sender" close to done. When I listen to the demo he's recorded in his garage during a storm the night before, I can hear the sound of the rain on the roof pounding a sense of catharsis into the song. Sometimes songs take different shapes as they evolve, and this one has become about expressing pain, or joy, or just what is . . . and how maybe, hopefully, that's enough.

*   *   *

For the Sender
hello my friend
it's me again
writing words i cannot send you

autumn's cold
the leaves are old
and letting go but not me

cause it's when we met
and it's when you left

and it's when our love was the best
so every year i write you this letter
but like a prayer
it's more for the sender
do you remember

sometimes i swear
you're in the air
am i just a great pretender

am i alone
i want to know
if you remember

it's when we met
and it's when you left
and it's when our love was the best
so every year i write you this letter
but like a prayer
it's more for the sender

do you remember
do you remember
do you remember
do you remember

A few days later I set up a small recording studio down-stairs in my living room with my laptop, some microphones, and a piece of equipment I buy on Craigslist. We record another version of "For the Sender" and I send the song to Emily as a thank-you for sending the letters to me. The next morning I get a note from her.

> *I smiled this big once . . . when I met him.*
> *I cried this hard once . . . when I lost him.*
> *After hearing this song, I am doing them both at once and loving every second of it.*
> *Never have I heard something so beautiful. I am in awe and feeling so . . . well . . . there's just no words, except I think I now know what heaven sounds like.*
> *Thank you.*
> *Emily*

I want to somehow make her feel that way again. I want to make her smile and cry and love deeply and completely, even if just for a moment. I want to make her feel that way because I want to feel that way, too.

So I write another song for her called "My Love Will Find You," about those first moments of reading her letter when the air caught in my throat. Her words "I'm one of the lucky ones" remind me of the poem by Tennyson, about it being better to have loved and lost than to have never loved at all. I imagine Emily moving through her days, speaking to her lost love, and sometimes hearing him tell her that he's there in the small moments. When she's feeling lost, his love will find her.

As I write the lyrics I keep hearing Jordan's powerful voice singing the choruses in my head. I make up my mind to find him at the next neighborhood family dinner and ask him to sing the song. He's hard not to find because he's a tall guy, on his way to being a tattoo artist, who has run out of space to practice on himself. He's sitting on the couch and shows me drawings he's recently done. They are beautifully intricate and seem to speak the way art does when words aren't enough.

I tell him about the song and ask if he'd like to sing the choruses. He nods his head and asks to hear it and I say, "Hang on a minute" and walk casually out the door, like it's no big deal. But as soon as I hit the driveway, I frantically run across the street, explode into my house, and grab my guitar and the lyrics, which I've written down earlier that day on a used piece of computer paper. I rush back to my neighbor's house and try to open the front door as calmly as I closed it. I hand Jordan the words and start to play the guitar while he sits on the couch and sings off the crumpled page, just like I heard the words in my head.

He says he'll sing the song as soon as I have the music done, so I call the band I've put together to play shows and record songs in San Diego. I've met some of the musicians here in town while wading slowly into San Diego's musical waters, and a few other guys I know from Seattle, where we waited for some kind of break in the rain before relocating to Southern California. I start calling them the Naysayers, because we are all a little jaded from the wait.

We record the music downstairs with my simple studio gear, and Jordan comes over to sing the choruses on a microphone set up in my entryway. He raises his arms triumphantly in the air as he sings "Shining down out loud," and I can feel the whole song lift with his energy.

I don't know who to ask to sing Emily's voice in the verses until the night I play on the same bill with Molly Jenson at the Belly Up Tavern. I tell her that I love the way she sings when we meet backstage, but I don't know her well enough yet to ask.

A few weeks later, however, she's at my house. She's a friend of Sean's, and he's asked her to sing a last-minute harmony on "For the Sender." I play her "My Love Will Find You" while she's here to see if she'd like to sing that one, too. She says she'd love to help, and as she sings, I quietly sense that some part of the song will somehow manifest in my own life. But it's a passing thought, and by the time Molly's done, I forget I ever had it.

*   *   *

My Love Will Find You

under amber autumn sky
forever never say goodbye
you held me close darling don't you cry
to love at all is the reason why

when you breathe i'm breathing inside you
when you run i'm running behind you (you said)
when you're feeling lost in the crowd
my love will find you

another autumn come undone
i still surrender the love we won
to the pages of tennyson
who loves at all is the lucky one

when you breathe i'm breathing inside you (i breathe)
when you run i'm running behind you (i run)
when you're feeling lost in the crowd
my love will find you
when you sleep i'm dreaming your gray skies blue (i sleep to dream)
shining down out loud
my love will find you

in sky blue
i find you,
you

ever since you went away
i try to smile my way through the day
i wrote you this letter to tell you i remember
and on this autumn wind i still hear you say

when you breathe i'm breathing inside you
when you run i'm running behind you (you said)
when you're feeling lost in the crowd
my love will find you
when you sleep i'm dreaming your gray skies blue (i sleep to dream)
shining down out loud
my love will find you

when you cry i'm crying inside you (i cry)
when you stand i'm standing beside you (i stand)
when you need a beautiful sign
i will remind you
when you sleep i'm dreaming your gray skies blue (i sleep)
shining down out loud
my love will find you
my love will find you
my love will find
my love will find
my love will find
you

* * *

Emily's Anno

I've been writing and singing about myself for so long that, listening back to those two songs later that night, I realize that it's the first time I've written and recorded someone else's voice singing someone else's story. In this new anonymity I begin to feel lighter and free, like a door has opened into a bright, airy room I've never seen, one that's been in my house the whole time but I always just walked past.

And now that I'm in the room, I don't want to leave, so I start another song about Emily's letter. One morning out in the water I ask Jon Foreman to come over and help me finish it. Jon and I are surfing together more often since that first family dinner, and when I paddle next to him he reaches his hand out, looks me in the eye, and asks how I am. And I know he means it. Small things like this tell me that Jon may be a great surfer and inspiring songwriter, but he's a better person.

He walks around the living room singing melodies and phrases as I play him the music I've come up with so far, and within a few minutes he hits on a chorus tag of "you are never alone." We finish the rest of the song over email while he's on the road, and I record the music downstairs with the Naysayers. I wait for Jon to come home for Christmas so we can record his vocal, but the holidays come and go and he gets backlogged with commitments before going back into the studio to work on the next Switchfoot album. I'm disappointed because I want to stay anonymous in the song and I think Jon could deliver a way better vocal than me, but after a couple weeks of waiting I abandon hope and head downstairs to sing it myself.

As I'm setting up to record my vocal, I get a phone call from Jon. I haven't spoken with him since our New Year's Eve family dinner, but he calls en route to Switchfoot's studio for their first day of recording. He says he'll be here in five minutes to sing our song, so I frantically search around for a pop screen, which is sort of a necessary noise-reducing mesh filter for the microphone. I can't find one so I have to improvise, and 15 minutes later Jon is singing "Never Alone" into pantyhose wrapped around a wire hanger.

* * *

Never Alone

we watched the western sky
falling like a landslide
we saw the half-light disappear
i know how it hurts inside
to watch the dead leaves dry
on your own year after year

i would never leave you
i would never leave you
even in your pain
you are never alone
you are never alone

we walk the streets tonight
lost in the tears we cried
for these dead and dying years
i can feel your heart beat running
i know we're not home yet honey
but let your hopes outweigh your fears

because i would never leave you
i would never leave you

even in your pain
you are never alone

can you hear my heart beat
can you hear my heart beat
can you hear my heart beat
can you hear my heart beat
keep running
can you hear my heart beat keep running
can you hear my heart beat keep running
can you hear my heart beat keep running
can you hear my heart beat

i would never leave you
i would never leave you
even in your pain
you are never alone

i would never leave you
i would never leave you
even in your pain
you are never alone
you are never alone
never alone
you are never alone

*   *   *

The air begins to change that winter. One night I'm standing on my roof, looking at the waves, with my arms wrapped around myself. I lean against the wind with my eyes closed and pretend I have on that imaginary coat I created back in Seattle, but it doesn't help much against actual weather.

As I open my eyes, I notice the lights shimmering off the Oceanside Pier in the distance. I've stood on this roof countless times but never really noticed the way the lights dance through the ocean spray. And I don't know if I haven't been quite as aware of my surroundings until now or if something really is different, but I'm somehow breathing a little deeper and feeling more present than before, more here right now instead of trying to be someplace else.

The textured light glinting off the waves reminds me of the way rustling leaves look in autumn's windswept trees. I remember watching the leaves let loose from their branches a little over a year ago and wishing that I could let go of *someday* as easily as the trees were letting go of their leaves.

I don't know that I've already begun.

It was still dark when he awoke, and, looking up,
he could see the stars through the half-destroyed roof.

— *The Alchemist*

THE SHELTER

Dear Alex:

I wanted to share
with you. I am not a wr
I know how to articulate
I do my best.

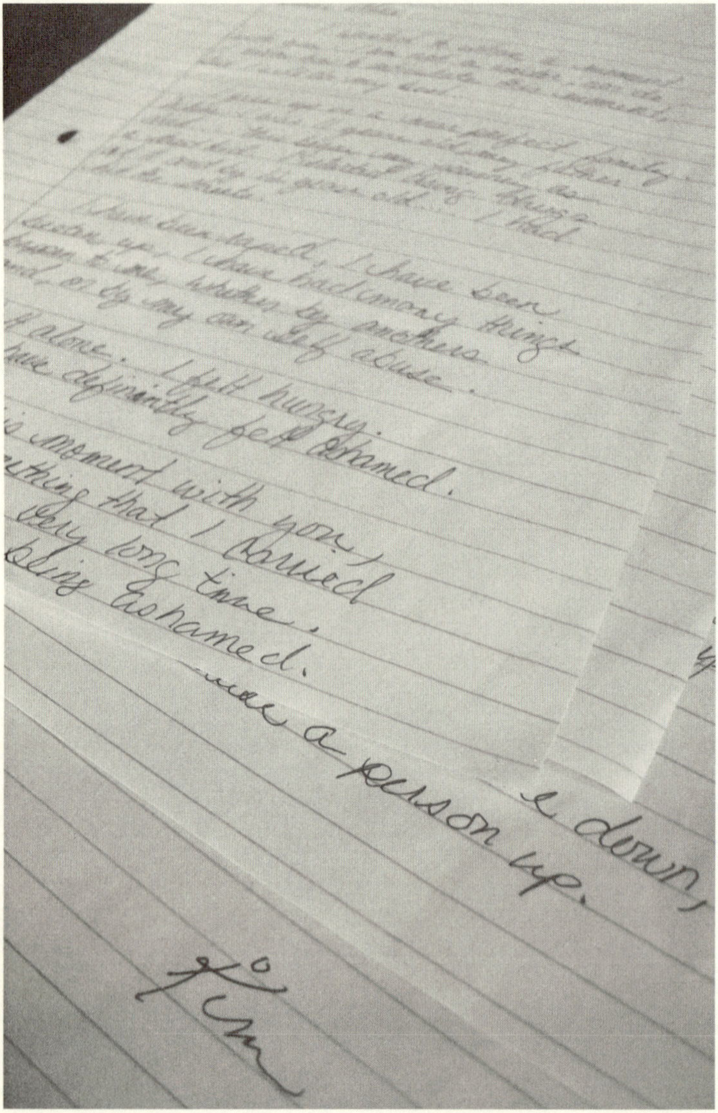

That stretch of shimmering San Diego coastline is a world away from Seattle, where a few years earlier I rent my little house overlooking the Space Needle to a mutual friend. So many moments and mistakes, so much growing happened in that house in my 20s, that I have a hard time letting go and allowing renters to make it their own.

Soon after my move to Southern California, I get a call from a neighbor in Seattle who says that I should come back immediately because something isn't right. She has been watching people come and go from the house at all hours and feels an overwhelming sense of darkness surrounding the place, which she can't explain without stuttering on the phone, but it's enough to get me and Kona in the truck and driving by morning.

Twenty-four hours farther north I take a left on Highland Drive from Fifth Avenue, head up Queen Anne Hill, and don't recognize what used to be my home. I park in the driveway, leave Kona in the truck, and walk through the trash littering the path. I knock on the door and no one answers, so I pause for a moment, wondering what I should do. I ask myself if I really want to open this door. *I don't live here anymore.* But with one hand on the door, I slowly push down on the unlocked handle.

I let myself into the shell of a house with an overwhelming sense of dead, unburied dreams suspended in the weak light filtering through the covered windows. Scattered among the piles of dirty napkins, sleeping bags, and Styrofoam take-out containers are hypodermic needles and antiseptic swabs. I've seen this house in movies and on the news, the one with the well dug in the basement and tunnels burrowed through the trash, the one I thought every town probably had but never thought would be mine.

I leave multiple messages for my tenant, telling him to get over here and get his stuff out, all the while thinking I should have known better: the missed rent payment in the first month, the little white lies, the disappearing act. But when I replay photographic moments of meeting him and his wife, she is nice in a wholesome, Midwestern kind of way, and he has a high-paying job, an Acura, and an affable sense of selling himself that makes him hard not to like.

By the time I walk through the house a couple of months later, her family has come to rescue her, and he finally shows up only to disappear into the bathroom for hours at a time to shoot up and pass out, when he is supposed to be getting his world out of mine. So while he's high and asleep on the toilet, I begin to do it myself.

I don't let Kona in the house for fear of her stepping on syringes, since it's hard to see with the windows either blacked out with paint or covered with tapestries. Underneath the sink I find a cut-off tangle of hair that feels like a wig, which I hold for a moment too long before realizing it's not a wig. There are burn marks all over the carpet upstairs from cooking cocaine and heroin together, which he's injecting every other hour and, while he won't let his wife shoot the speedballs, he does let her smoke them. He tells me a month before that he has a passing affinity for weed, which he promises to only smoke outside. He doesn't mention what might happen inside.

I move all of his stuff out and pile his stained furniture and clothes on the front porch, because I can't get anything into the garage, which is already packed with boxes and syringes. There's barely room for me to wonder how this happened to my little house, the little house where I spent Christmases and had fires in the woodstove on Sundays. I'll never know what really happened here, but as I walk through the rooms with my shirt pulled up over my nose, picking up needles and dropping tears, the walls tell me in their own way that it's better I don't know.

This house is sacred to me for many reasons, and while I've heard it's because I'm a Cancer, I think it's mostly because this is where I spent so many nights with Kona at my feet, trying to find my place in the world outside the rain-streaked windows of my 20s. This house was my shelter.

This was my home.

But I will never spend another night here, and it will never be my home again. Instead, it offers me a portal into addiction and my own sense of loss of place and belonging, which I won't experience as deeply again until I play a benefit back in San Diego with Jon's band a few summers later. Proceeds from the Switchfoot Bro-Am go to a local homeless shelter for kids, some of whom are already fighting addiction, and Jon and I visit the shelter later that summer.

We play guitars, hang out with the kids, and bring Jordan with us the next time. One kid is a former professional bull rider, and he lifts up his shirt to show me the scar on his belly from a longhorn. He says he got hurt and can't ride anymore, then glances at my guitar and says he'd sure like to hear a country song. I ask him which one, and he runs back into the shelter's office to get an old ghetto blaster. There's a Garth Brooks CD inside the player, and he starts singing along with one of the tracks while the indie-rock kids look at him sideways. I tell him I can't do better than Garth, but I sure can play some Johnny Cash. He smiles and says that's good enough for him.

In and out of playing songs we hear young stories of isolation, overwhelming loss, alcohol and drug abuse, bad decisions, and the deepest pains of growing up alone and afraid. Kim, the director of the shelter, tells me privately that the teenage bull rider enlisted in the Marines after he got hurt. He was sent to Iraq but went AWOL after his first tour of duty because he wasn't prepared for what he saw in battle. The first chance he had, he ran.

He is still running when we meet him that day at the shelter. Kim convinces him to turn himself in a few weeks later, and says she will be there for him when he's released, because he sacrificed his life for all of us while trying to make a better one for himself.

The week after our visit I get a note from Kim.

Jon and Alex . . .

I can't thank you enough for taking time out of your schedule to come down and just "chill" with the kids. I didn't tell the kids or the volunteers that you were coming. I hope that was okay. I didn't want it to be "false" in any way. I just wanted you to be guys coming down to hang out with the kids.

Although . . . I know a number of them knew who you were immediately! Once again, your gift of time has really touched the kids' lives. They will revel in the memories that they hung out with you, Jessica most of all. I couldn't slap the grin off that girl's face . . . nor would I ever want to.

They played it "cool" while you were here, but it was ALL A BUZZ when you left! Thank you for that precious gift.

I gave you a hurried tour (and I am so sorry) as the center was gearing up to open and there are so many little things to care for. I hope you saw what a difference you have made to our little center. We are able to offer SO MUCH more to the kids than just food and clothing now. We have taken the gift that you gave us last year and have run, run, run with it.

Thanks . . . from the deepest place in my heart.

- Kim G.

Alex and Jon at the shelter

I wonder what kind of road led Kim to be the director of a homeless shelter for kids, so I write back to her and ask. A letter shows up not long after, written on lined notebook paper, with an answer I'm not expecting.

Dear Alex,

I wanted to share a moment with you. I am not a writer, nor do I know how to articulate this moment, but I will do my best.

I grew up in a near perfect family . . . when I was 11 years old, my father died . . . this began my journey as a street kid. I started using drugs at 11 and by 12 years old . . . I had hit the streets. I had been raped, I had been beaten up, I had many things happen to me, whether by another's hand, or by my own self-abuse. I felt alone. I felt hungry. I definitely felt ashamed.

I share with you this moment, as it was something that I carried with me for a long time. That feeling of being ashamed. Of being so ugly and hideous, that no one could possibly love me . . . I didn't love me. I made myself ugly on the outside, too. My story is no different than many of the kids that are out there right now.

What I remember most are the acts of random people, strangers many of them, people I will never be able to thank. They would sit there and stare at me, with all my ugliness that I openly wore and tell me . . .

"Why do you do this? You are beautiful . . ."

I didn't feel beautiful.

"You are so smart, why are you wasting yourself?"

I didn't feel smart, would a smart person be in this situation?

"Darling . . . you are SO SPECIAL."

I didn't feel special.

It was these random acts of kindness that changed me on the inside. It began as a whisper, "Maybe I am beautiful . . . maybe I am smart . . . maybe, just maybe . . . I am special."

From there, the inner voice grew in strength. You are beautiful! You are smart! YOU ARE SPECIAL!

These "angels" as I call them, changed my world. They helped me change the way I viewed myself. People don't realize the power of the spoken word . . . it can be used to tear someone down, but it can also raise up a person's spirit, especially, when that spirit is so broken, that it can't hold itself up. I thank those people for holding me up and giving me time to heal, as my spirit is strong now . . . and I hope that I can help hold someone else's spirit, while their spirit heals.

When I say to one of my kids, "You are special," I mean it . . . I am holding up that little girl I was before, and loving her, each time I love one of the kids . . . and my kids, they are beautiful, and they are special, and they deserve to be treated with dignity, not pity. As I deserved to be treated with dignity.

Anyone can change the world. It begins with the simple act of kindness, it begins from within.

- Kim

A few weeks later, Jon and I are trading waves and talking about writing a song based on Kim's letter and our experience with the kids at the shelter. He leaves soon for another tour with Switchfoot and sends me a demo for "Unbroken" from the road. I can hear the power of the song through the scratchy recording, and I hesitate before sending him any writing suggestions. It doesn't really need any changes, so for the first time with any song I've been involved in, I take myself out of the writing loop.

Instead, I record the drums, acoustic guitar, and background vocals in my living room and send it to Jon to add his own tracks. One afternoon when he is back home, we finish up overdubs at the Switchfoot studio, and as we listen to the song over the studio speakers, I sense a certain unassailable strength in his voice, a defiant hope amidst the pain and uncertainty that hung in the air at the shelter.

*   *   *

Unbroken

out on the margins of town
i been stuck hanging round
these amateur clowns
wondering where were you
the only song we knew
was our amateur blues

if you believed why'd you leave me
if you believed why'd you leave me
even after sticks and stones were spoken
i'm alive
i'm alive

and i'm unbroken
i'm unbroken

i been abused and misled
i been stuck in my head
unsung and unsaid
been on needles and thread
i been left for dead
but i'm living instead

if you believed why'd you leave me
if you believed why'd you leave me
even after sticks and stones were spoken
i'm alive
i'm alive
and i'm unbroken
i'm unbroken

give me a song to sing
something to balance out
the fits and starts
that life can bring
i'm waiting
give me a song to sing
a decent melody
because i'm alone and i'm nineteen
and i feel like the world

is trying to swallow me whole
like it's trying to swallow me whole

if you believed why'd you leave me
if you believed why'd you leave me
even after our sticks and stones were spoken
i'm alive
i'm alive
and i'm unbroken
yeah i'm unbroken
i'm unbroken
i'm alive
and i'm unbroken

*   *   *

It's early the next morning, and I'm watching the soft light catch the dust as it breaks through the living room window. I'm starting to find more grace in writing about other people's stories than my own, and I play simple chords as I replay Kim's words about hearing that small voice telling her she was beautiful. By the second cup of coffee, "Love Began As a Whisper" goes from a street corner to the house where love lives, up the front steps and to the front door, where a fateful moment waits.

I record a quick version of the song so I don't forget it, and as I listen back to the lyric "one hand on the trigger, one hand on the door," I feel as if I've had that same moment of pause and not known it. It's not the action itself, it's that space of decision just before; my addict tenant took a breath in and out before he took his first hit of anything, and the homeless teenage bull rider took the same kind of breath before he went AWOL.

Maybe everybody has those moments, that breath just before we take the drink or walk away, keep the baby or end the marriage, start over or end it all ourselves. Whatever it is, it's one hand on the trigger, one hand on the door.

Molly comes by a couple of days later to sing harmony on my vocal for "Love Began As a Whisper." I feel very connected to my voice in the song and only want her to sing backup, but she starts singing my melody while my lead vocal is muted in the recording session. I let the track run to see what happens, and when she sings the first line of the second verse I feel like I'm suspended in that moment between tripping and catching my fall, that space where my breath is caught in my throat but I know I'm going to be okay. She brings my words a more beautiful life than I ever could have given them, and it is my biggest lesson yet in letting go musically. I'm no longer tethered to my voice singing something I wrote, and the song is better for it.

Love Began As a Whisper

love began as a whisper
from under the door
locking a house where
i don't live no more
i'm here on the porch stair
in my ugly coat
love began as a whisper
and it started to grow

you are beautiful
and you're almost home

from a lonesome corner
with no place to go
those words were my streetlights
leading me home
while hunger and shame were
holding hands with hope
love began as a whisper
and started to grow

you are beautiful
so beautiful
and you're almost home

so i crawled the last mile to
love's front door
but now i hear nothing
but the symphony roar
one hand on the trigger
one hand on the door
is this the moment
i been waiting for
one hand on the trigger
one hand on the door

you are beautiful
so beautiful
you are beautiful

*　　*　　*

I ask Jordan to come over and sing *a cappella* harmony on "Love Began As a Whisper," and after he's done we kick around the idea of doing a song together about Kim's letter, since he was at the shelter with Jon and me. He wants to do something different musically than what he's used to doing with New Found Glory, something more alternative-country. Those are waters I've been treading for years, so while he's on the road a few weeks later I get the music done with the Naysayers for "The Right Words." The lyrics take shape around the music until Jordan comes by one morning to sing the song into the microphone set up in my entryway.

While his voice bounces off the vaulted ceiling, I lean forward on my elbows, put my head in my hands, and wonder where all of this is heading. The songs and letters together seem like they're growing into something else, something bigger than the sum of their parts. Maybe we could make this some sort of benefit project and give money from the songs to causes chosen by the letter writers. There would be so many moving parts and so many questions, and I would need the kind of help I'm not used to asking for.

Under my breath I tell myself to stay out of the way and trust the process. Lately I'm finding that sometimes what I want isn't really what I need, and the right things seem to happen if I'm patient. These last few songs plant a seed for that kind of trust in the way things work, because I've had to take careful, slow steps in between everyone's different touring and recording schedules. So over the last few months, when my plane is late, or I don't get a phone call back, or I don't get the gig, I measure my reaction and take a breath. It seems to make sense later if I let it.

Jordan's voice echoing around the house brings me back to the present moment, and as the song ends I hit the STOP button and listen back. We never know if he gets off the streets in the song, but there is a sense of cleansing and renewal. And hope.

*　　*　　*

The Right Words
couldn't think of the right words to say
don't know if it mattered that much anyway

i can't believe that it's already been a week
i'm alright i finally got something to eat
and ok 'cause i found a place to sleep
'cause it gets hard
when it gets dark

but i can see
what i'm doing to me
i couldn't breathe when i
couldn't think of the right words to say
don't know if it mattered that much anyway
you wouldn't change so i couldn't stay
don't know if i mattered that much anyway

now i'm here just living on the streets
i sell myself while i get my kicks for free
don't know who i was when i was me

and it got hard
when it got dark
but i could see
what it was doing to me
i couldn't breathe when i
couldn't think of the right words to say
don't know if it mattered that much anyway
you wouldn't change so i couldn't stay
don't know if i mattered that much anyway

and then you came around
the right words
make such a beautiful sound
you are beautiful
you are beautiful

make me over
washing myself clean
and now i'm finding the right words say
learning what matters at the end of the day
found a place where my soul can stay
and change for the better a little more every day
now I'm finding the right words to say
now I'm finding the right words to say

*   *   *

A few days go by and I have lunch with Kim, who begins to cry as I tell her how we've reimagined her letter. I say I want to donate money from the songs to her shelter but I don't yet know what shape it will take, and she says we could change people's lives through these songs without a dime ever being given. As she talks a couple of tears drip off her nose and onto the table. The purity of her emotion hits me unexpectedly, and I have to hold myself back from crying, too. As I listen to her, I can feel my defenses falling down and my heart opening up to how I used to be before I needed a make-believe coat to keep the dreams in and reality out.

The winter sun shines bright as I squint through my windshield on the drive home, thinking about how there is so much emotion still hidden behind that coat of protection that I've forgotten what certain deep moments feel like. The imaginary fabric may buffer me from cold realities, but I pull into the driveway knowing that a coat makes it hard to feel the sunlight on my skin.

As I walk in the house, I imagine hanging the coat on the rack by the front door. I sleep a dreamless sleep that night and wake up the next morning to find it in a metaphor of tatters on the floor.

I light the remaining patches of fabric on fire in my mind and close my eyes to watch the pile burn until there are only ashes and smoke. And I head down to the beach with my coffee, through the early February mist in nothing but jeans and a T-shirt.

I says, "What's this call, this sperit?" An I says, "It's love. . . .
Why do we got to hang it on God or Jesus?"

— *The Grapes of Wrath*

THE SEARCH

Dear Alex:

I wanted to share
with you. I am not a w
I know how to articulate
I do my best.

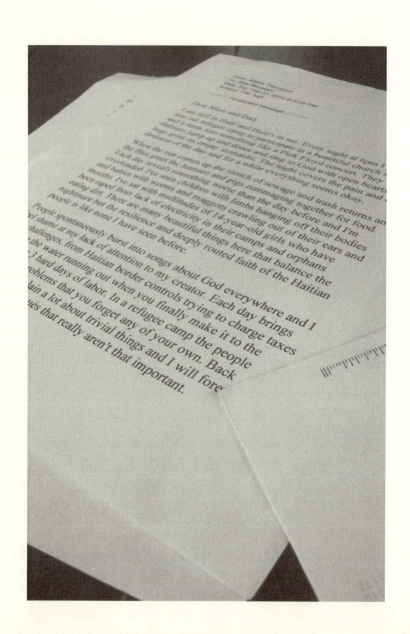

Dear Mom and Dad,

I am still in Haiti and Haiti's in me. Every night at 6pm I go to a refugee camp to participate in a beautiful church s... and it turns into something like a Pink Floyd concert. They Haitian jump up and down and sing to God with open hearts... big grins on empty stomachs. The night covers the pain and ... dirtiness of the day and for a while everything seems okay.

When the sun comes up the stench of sewage and trash returns an... the flies greet the humans and pigs rummaging together for food. Each day reveals something worse than the day before and I'm overloaded. I've seen children with limbs hanging off their ears and and babies with worms and maggots crawling out of their bodies mouths. I've sat with multitudes of 14-year-old girls who have been raped from lack of electricity in their camps and orphans eating dirt. There are many beautiful things here that balance the nightmare but the resilience and deeply routed faith of the Haitian people is like none I have seen before.

People spontaneously burst into songs about God everywhere and I feel shame at my lack of attention to my creator. Each day brings challenges, from Haitian border controls trying to charge taxes to the water running out when you finally make it to the ...3 hard days of labor. In a refugee camp the people ...roblems that you forget any of your own. Back ...lain a lot about trivial things and I will fore ...ues that really aren't that important.

Long Beach, California, has a particular smell. It is the smell of my childhood, strong with exhaust from the street traffic on Park Avenue and vapors from the evening dew evaporating in the midmorning sun. I can feel the heat coming off the stucco on the 1930s Spanish-style houses in my old neighborhood as I wait for my grandma to answer the door to her duplex, just across the street from where I grew up.

She opens the door with wet eyes that tell me she's either been sleeping or crying. I hug and kiss her on the way in, and before long she asks me if I have seen the new back office. I have seen it, sat in it, and talked with her in it for the last couple of years, but she can't remember those kinds of things anymore.

We are waiting for her old Steck player piano to be delivered from my house in Seattle, the house that used to be my home but is now sitting empty save the scorch marks and darkness left in the addicts' wake. Her piano followed me north to Seattle and is now following me back to Southern California and a temporary resting place in her duplex. I have played and written songs on that piano since I was a boy, when I would spend Saturday nights at Grandma's house, sleeping in the twin bed next to her and pounding out chords with tiny fists after Bisquick pancakes on Sunday mornings.

"I'll see you in a little while," she says as she shuffles off to take a nap. She is hardly moving at all now, but soon enough she will be confined to her bed forever, wearing diapers and breaking into songs like "It's 3 O'clock in the Morning" mid-sentence. I walk back into the living room where Kona is also napping, waking only to thump her tail in acknowledgment before falling back into her own dreams.

I hear the moving truck's air brakes pumping out on Park Avenue and walk to the window in time to see the piano rolling down the truck's ramp. A melody wanders into my mind, and I remember writing a song for my grandma on that piano just before they loaded it onto the truck in Seattle. I called it "The Invitation," because my grandma has been dying for years, and I feel like she's been holding in her hands an invitation to get into heaven, but for some reason God won't let her into the party.

The movers lug the piano into the house, and by the time they position it in the corner, both Kona and my grandma wake up from their naps. I sign for the delivery, and after some wandering conversation, I get my grandma a glass of milk, give her a hug, and put Kona in my truck. As I drive away, I can see my grandma in the window, staring out and holding her milk, and I wish I could rescue her from the confines of that duplex and her fading consciousness. I wish I could put her in the back of my truck and take her to heaven or wherever it is she's supposed to go. All of her friends are already there, including the love of her life, but she is still locked out, lying in her bed, year after year, unable to remember, but completely able to feel pain. Still alive, but not.

On the drive home I find myself thinking that if there were a just God, he would have allowed my grandma a graceful exit years ago instead of making her stand outside the gates as she turns into a puddle of what she once was. I have these questioning conversations *about* God with myself quite often when I'm in the water or driving long stretches of highway. But rarely do I have any kind of conversation *with* God, and if I do, it's never part of a church service.

I inherit this tenuous relationship with a higher power and religion from my mom, who probably learned it from my grandma. My grandma is full of lessons, both in life and word, but few have anything to do with a higher power. One of her favorite sayings is, "Money isn't everything, but it sure as hell helps," which says to me that faith in herself won out over faith in God as she ground through the Depression. She tells me stories of growing up poor in the 1920s and '30s and how her mom, a cafeteria worker named Clara, fed the family whatever leftovers she could bring home from work. Clara was also a seamstress and made my grandma's underwear from the cafeteria's burlap potato sacks. This was life in Depression-era Southern California, and from my grandma's burlap underwear I think I understand poverty with gritty grace.

As my grandma disintegrates over the next few years, she often stares off into nothing, lost in another world where she doesn't recognize me or remember her name. But sometimes when I ask her about the past, she'll come back to who she used to be and talk about yesteryear like it was yesterday.

There is no mention of God when she talks about the car wreck that changed my grandfather forever and took away his trucking business, no mention of God in her stories of leaving him and struggling to feed my mom and aunt. The only time I hear her talk about God is when she says she couldn't wait on God when there were mouths to feed. And there is no mention at all of her leaving my mom and aunt in a Masonic orphanage, where they develop their own suspicions of any God who would cause a car wreck or allow children to go hungry. Or take their childhood and shove it in the broom closet of an orphanage.

Despite my mom's firm atheism, I get a sense as a kid of something bigger than myself from the congregational church down the street, where my parents send me to keep me out of trouble and gain some moral grounding. As I grow up, I grow out of the belief that there is only one correct religion, but I still feel spiritually grounded through my connection to the ocean and a shelf full of books by the great teachers. I come to believe that there is a way things work, and that way can be called God, or Love, or the Tao, or the Way, or whatever. As I get older, I find that most religions seem to hold the same few beautiful laws for living, and what I call it doesn't really matter anyway, as long as I try to live it. Easier said than done.

A few years after the piano delivery in Long Beach, my grandma is suffering even more. We are unsure when she will

i need you to come to my rescue
(i will be your) i need you (hallelujah)

sometimes i can hear voices
coming from up above
sometimes they sound like sirens
sometimes they sound like love (hello)
but all i see is darkness
and i don't feel no light
and nobody's asking if i'm alright

i need you to come to my rescue
(i will be your) i need you (hallelujah)
ain't there anything you can do
to come to my rescue

now i can't tell if it's heaven
but there's a light drawing near
and i can't tell if i'm flying
(i will be your)
or if i'm still lying here
(hallelujah)
then i see shadows around me
(so hold on darling)
i hear a dog somewhere
(i am coming)

finally be relieved of her time here, so I find room for the piano
in San Diego. The morning before we load it into the house,
I read a charged story in the paper about church leaders con-
demning the right-to-die movement and suggesting we follow
God's plan. This adds layers to my frustration, and I wonder if
those intent on calling religion only one thing are the ones who
need to live it better, and the louder they speak, yelling at each
other on TV shows, the more they can't hear themselves.

Around Christmastime, images start coming over the
airwaves of an earthquake quickly turning into a humanitar-
ian crisis in Haiti. I am asked to contribute a song to a benefit
record, so I write and record "Rescue," which echoes my
spiritual search and tries to imagine some sort of answer. You
can see God at work in the cleanup, but it's tough to see any
sign of Him in the devastation.

*   *   *

Rescue

i don't know how i got here
i don't know what i done
i only know i been buried
where the end has begun
because all i see is darkness
and i don't see no light
and nobody's asking if i'm alright

i feel arms around me
(can you hold on somehow)
and a change in the air
(it won't be long now)
then i am out of the darkness
(i need you to be)
and i am into the light
(singing with me)
somebody's asking am i
(hallelujah)
somebody's asking am i
(hallelujah)
i hear you asking
are you alright

*   *   *

A video of relief efforts paired with the song makes it onto the Facebook page of Alison Thompson, a medic for Sean Penn's foundation in Haiti. Alison was also a first responder to 9/11, instrumental in the Southeast Asia tsunami relief, and, as I soon learn, a beautiful woman committed to serving humanity in beautiful ways. A colonel logs her in at the Special Ops tent outside Port-au-Prince, and she sends me an email after seeing the video.

Alison

Alison Thompson, February 16 at 8:33 AM
*I just went to the colonel and he let me see it on their special
ops Internet . . . it is really beautiful and is really accurate to what
is going on here. Thank you, thank you—really beautiful. I started
crying, as I have been here so long I haven't seen outside images
to the world. . . . We are so tired (the workers and volunteers).
Yesterday I vomited all night and was dizzy all day due to
exhaustion and took 3 IVs into my body. . . . it's been a long and
hard journey and a long way to go. Thank you for doing this . . . .*

I'm only helping in the small ways I know how, but this
thank-you note from Alison is the third I've received lately,

three more than I can remember getting in a long time. The other two notes from Emily and Kim inspire me to dig deeper and eventually give rise to songs, so I ask Alison to tell me more about what it's really like there. While there is very little communication in and out of Haiti in the few weeks after the earthquake strikes, she gets access to special ops Internet again and forwards me a letter she wrote home to her parents in Australia.

> *Dear Mum and Dad,*
>
> *I am still in Haiti and Haiti's in me. Every night I go down into our refugee camp to participate in a beautiful church service and it turns into something like a Pink Floyd concert. The Haitians jump up and down and sing to God with open hearts and huge grins on empty stomachs. The night covers the pain and the dirtiness of the day, and for a while everything seems okay. When the sun comes up the stench of sewage and trash returns, and the flies greet the humans and pigs rummaging together for food. Each day reveals something worse than the day before and I'm overloaded. I've seen children with limbs hanging off their bodies and babies with worms and maggots crawling out of their ears and mouths. I've sat with multitudes of 14-year-old girls who have been raped from lack of electricity in their camps, and orphans eating dirt.*
>
> *There are many beautiful things here that balance the nightmare, but the resilience and deeply routed faith of the*

Haitian people is like none I have seen before. People spontane-ously burst into songs about God everywhere, and I feel shame at my lack of attention to my creator. Each day brings new challenges from Haitian border control trying to charge taxes for aid on the water already running out, when I finally make it to the shower after 3 hard days of labor. The people here in the refugee camp have so many problems that you forget any of your own. Back home people complain a lot about trivial things and I will forever learn to be quiet on issues that really aren't that important.

The American Army 82nd Airborne have been superheroes. They have saved thousands of lives with food, tents, security, and medical help. I have had the privilege to get to know the 82nd Grey Falcons on a daily individual basis and am blown away by their intelligence and caring quiet natures. L. Colonel Foster, L. Colonel McFayden, Major Jordan, and Major El-dredge lead a swarm of gentlemen who talk daily of their wives and families and how they love their country. I've never seen this side of Army life before but feel honored to have worked side by side with some of the greatest men I have ever met. The Haitian people are begging the American Army to stay and help. They are very scared of what will happen when they leave. I know the Americans can't stay and hold their hand forever but maybe they can for a few more sunsets?

xx Alison

I feel love in her words about sewage and rape and faith, because the simple act of her being there to help is the purest form of love I can imagine. After reading her letter I think, *If there is a God, He might rather be called something else. Something like Love.*

Sometimes I see my neighbor Jack Tempchin walking down my street. He isn't yet part of our family dinners, but I know who he is: a legend, at least among songwriters. Jack is best known for writing the Eagles's "Peaceful Easy Feeling" back in the '70s, followed by a string of other hits. I think about saying hello once in a while as we pass each other, but I've never been very good at introductions, especially when it comes to introducing myself.

We finally meet one night at a bar out on Highway 101 when the girl I bring with me approaches Jack and tells him she's a fan. She is better looking than either Jack or me, and as she holds court neither of us can really focus much on conversation. Her interest in me doesn't last long past that night, but I've grown used to seeing people walk away, and after we have *the talk*, I turn my energy to writing about Alison's letter. But this time around, writing feels less like an excuse for being alone. It feels more like an honor.

I reach out to Jack to see if he's interested in writing with me, and can't quite believe it when he agrees and pulls up to the house one afternoon in what looks like a late '80s Crown Victoria. He comes to the door with an old Martin guitar and a pocketful of dog treats for Stella, my new hurricane of a Labrador doing her hellion best to fill the space left behind by Kona, who by now has been gone a little over a year.

Jon shows up to surf in front of the house as Stella is pillaging Jack's pockets for more dog treats. I invite him to write with us, but his window of water time is closing before he leaves on tour again. By the time he's drying off, "Act of God" is almost done. Jack's gentle way calms Stella down, and she lays at his feet while we record the song live in the living room.

I play it later for Jon over the studio speakers, his hair still wet from the ocean. He turns from the speakers after the last chord rings out and tells me that this is one of the only times he's ever wished he hadn't gone surfing, so he could have been in the room writing with us. I don't show it but I can feel myself light up inside, all the way to the backside of my heart.

My questions, and Jack's, too, come out in the song, which reflects the difficulty in reconciling this disaster with a higher power, as well as the ultimate surrender to the way things are. Maybe sometimes it just is what it is and we have to trust the process.

But that's easier said than done.

*   *   *

Act of God

i'm in the trouble and the trouble's in me
and there ain't no way to escape this reality
what i see blasts my eyes runs down my spine
like a lightning rod
but i don't know who to blame for it
because it's just an act of god

there's so much pain here but there's so much good
people do more beautiful things in times of trouble
than i ever thought they would
i said i really cared before but that was a façade
i guess you never know the truth
til you know an act of god

and if god makes the sunset and he makes the deep blue sea
he makes the earthquake the tornado
the typhoon the volcano and me
then my church is this ocean my sky this stained glass view
and my offering is this open hand brother that i'm holding out to you

now the trouble's half a world away but
the trouble's still in me
i came two thousand miles home to watch
the same sun setting in the sea

as I take the pen of yesterday
and I slowly start to draw
i can see the whole picture clear now
and it's all an act of god

if the master plan is perfect
i guess it's we who are flawed
when we don't understand the suffering
that's part of an act of god

*   *   *

I'm doing an early spring cleaning a couple of days later when I find a torn, yellowed piece of paper behind my desk with the words, "heart was broken wide open" scrawled in my hurried handwriting. I can't remember why I wrote those words down but the phrase reminds me of Alison's letter about the humanity, hope, and light she is seeing through the cracks of disaster, especially in the church services she describes.

She sends me a video of one of the services taken on her cell phone, and it captures all the energy in its shaky brilliance. People are dancing and praising and singing, somehow finding their God in the middle of an earthly hell, something I haven't even been able to do as an observer, much less a victim. I've sometimes played the victim, but I've never really been one. Not like that.

Sara Watkins is Sean's sister and sings like an angel, maybe because she kind of is one. I get to know her better over the last year after she hears through a neighbor about Kona dying and brings over a plumeria in a clay pot with a beautiful card. We surf together and laugh at a dozen family dinners before she lends her voice to a song of mine called "Reno," giving me one of my most special moments as a songwriter.

I invite her and Jack over to the house, and we start writing "Broken Wide Open" about the crack in Alison's heart that is letting the light in. We sit on the couch, Jack and I playing guitar and Sara with her notebook, and within a couple of hours we've almost finished the song. We track it a few days later downstairs, with Sara and I sharing a microphone and her brother Sean playing guitar.

I send the tracks to Rami Jaffee, who plays piano, accordion, and B3 organ on the song. I first saw Rami onstage with the Wallflowers back in Seattle, and he has since played with Pearl Jam and Foo Fighters and is a sought-after session player. I never imagined he'd play on something I was involved in, but a mutual friend tells him about the idea behind the song, and within a few days I'm listening to the first notes of his piano on "Broken Wide Open."

* * *

Broken Wide Open

never been so shattered i couldn't think
never been thirsty with no sweet water to drink
never been so alone with no friend to hold
never felt so much sorrow touching my soul

my heart was broken wide open
heaven let the light shine in
my heart was broken wide open
and i'll never be the same again
broken wide open

the night covers the pain and the dirt of the day
when angel voices sing my troubles away
blessings in disguise are hard to believe
it took a mountain falling on me
before I was ready to receive

my heart was broken wide open
heaven let the light shine in
my heart was broken wide open
and i'll never be the same again

been trying to find where
the wrong meets the right

we don't always know where that's at
what's gone is gone
it'll never come back
and i'll just have to live with that

my heart's been broken wide open
that let the light shine in
my heart's been broken wide open
and i'll never be the same again
broken wide open
broken wide open
broken wide open

*　　*　　*

The deeper that sorrow carves into your being,
the more joy you can contain.

— The Prophet

THE WELL

Dear Alex:

I wanted to share
with you. I am not a w
I know how to articulate
I know . . . I do my best.

Dear Alex—

Wyatt was born in late October [...]
than I thought was possible. Dan [...]
for several hours at night just [...]
After 2 months, I was pretty m[...]
rope. The baby wouldn't eat, d[...]
was sure I was failing as a [...]

Dan was working the nigh[...]
home on his break one nigh[...]
and calm me down. He told [...]
home with me if I needed [...]
want to admit that it was [...]
so I let him go back [...]

An hour or so later, I [...]
saying that a cop had b[...]
nervous but thought there [...]
be Danny. But after a [...]
on the door and I m[...]
best friend Richie who [...]
he had very close [...]
with friends, family, [...]
started gathering [...]
the hospital. At [...]
only shot in th[...]
visit him. But [...]
pulled me aside [...]
He told me Dan [...]

[...]
chang[...]
the [...]
wit[...]
had w[...]
Jordan [...]

Katelyn Groth

It's August, the month after my grandma's piano is delivered in Long Beach. My family is standing with a large group of people in the back room of a Mexican restaurant in Dallas. Some of us are more awkwardly using space than others, and my mom has her face turned into the shoulder of the new widower, hiding her emotion while sadness seeps around the room.

Sadness is like water held in a well, carved deep into the ground of everyday life. Sometimes the well is emptied suddenly, maybe by a car wreck or an unexpected fast-moving illness. The water dumps in sheets over the edge and onto the ground, and everyone left behind stands around waist deep in sadness doing what they can to get rid of it, when all they can really do is just wait.

But this well down in the Highland Park neighborhood of Dallas has been drawn out slowly, over a period of many years, and the water spilling over the edge has had plenty of time to sink back down into the ground. Traces of moisture seep around the edges of the Mexican restaurant, but only traces. The sadness here has been let out over the years as frustration and resignation, so by the time Grace dies, the well has almost run dry.

The next day I am ushered into the pews reserved for family and keep my eyes set straight ahead to avoid the standing-room-only crowd that has packed into the church. I wonder if anyone here knew what was really going on with Grace, and my frustration wants to stand up and tell some of these people that the world isn't as perfect as their makeup, but the family minister does it for me. His words take us from the church out

into a field somewhere, out past religion and all the noise that goes
with it, out where the truth is.

He tells the conservative Southern congregation that Grace
battled clinical depression for 20 years, that it almost tore her
family apart, that it did tear her marriage apart, and that she took
her own life. The preacher says that in the pain and loss there are
lessons of judgment, guilt, and love. But mostly love.

What hurts me most is seeing my sister cry, something
I have never seen before. We are in a courtyard outside the
church after the service, a very small group gathered to watch
Grace's ashes be placed into one of the walls. The family
minister says a few words to us, and then reads a note that
Grace left when she first tried to kill herself six years earlier.
The postscript reads "It's not your fault. Remember."

My nephew starts crying as our plane waits on the tarmac
at DFW, and I wonder why my brother-in-law isn't quieting
him down. I look across the aisle to see photocopied, handwritten pages being turned. It is the note from Grace, who has
left behind two sons, a daughter, grandchildren she knows,
grandchildren she will never know, and a widower going
through her belongings in a nice colonial in Highland Park.

I watch my brother-in-law turn the pages for a moment
before turning my head away to the window.

Grace was more than a statistic, more than a sympathetic
nod from a family friend, more than a box of ashes interred in
a church wall. She was his mom.

Flying over the outskirts of Dallas, I stare down at unfinished freeways that rise into nothing. They are under construction, connector roads and off-ramps that drop off into thin air, waiting for something or someone to complete them. There are cars racing on every road except the unfinished ones, and I wonder which road Grace was on, which road my grandma is on, which road the addict is on. And I wonder which road I am on, all the way back to San Diego.

A couple of years later, just before Christmas, a young police officer on a gang beat is shot and killed a few miles north of my town, leaving behind a widow and an infant son. As I watch the news broadcasts on continuous replay, I think about that well of sadness and how it's being emptied so suddenly with this young officer's death, which takes me back to Grace's slow suicide and flying over the unfinished roads outside Dallas.

The television noise fades away as my mind wanders off, and I think about how one of life's brutal ironies is that it is often taken too soon from someone doing something good in the world, someone who wants to be here, while someone like Grace has to take her own life, and my grandma isn't being allowed to die at all. I wonder where the God is in that and how a local hero's road—protecting community, going to

church, being a husband and dad—how a road like that ends
so suddenly, with an infant son hanging by his diaper on the
exposed rebar.

Maybe that's where God is. Somewhere in the rebar.

As the news goes to break, I realize that only a few weeks
before the shooting, the-soon-to-be widow, pregnant with their
son, had come by my house with a mutual friend. Her name
is Katelyn, and I remember being told she was married to a
police officer. I recognize her last name from the news footage
and make the connection while a *Charlie Brown Christmas* com-
mercial plays on TV.

A year and a half passes, and Katelyn's loss is drifting
away in the haze of my memory when I get a note from her
new husband, who knows Sara Watkins and has heard that we
are writing songs about letters. In passing, I wonder about the
short lapse between the officer's death and her new marriage,
but I understand better when I hear from Katelyn herself.

Dear Alex,

*Wyatt was born in late October and screamed more than I
thought was possible. Dan would drive him around for several
hours at night just to get him to sleep. After 2 months, I was
pretty much at the end of my rope. The baby wouldn't eat and
didn't sleep well, and I was sure I was failing as a mother.*

Dan was working the night shift, so he came home on his

break one night to cook me dinner and calm me down. He told me he would stay home with me if I needed him to, but I didn't want to admit that it was too much for me to handle, so I let him go back to work.

An hour or so later, I got a call from a friend saying that a cop had been shot. I got a little nervous but thought there was no way it could possibly be Danny. After a few minutes someone knocked on the door and I immediately felt ill. It was his best friend, Richie. He came to tell me that it was Dan who was shot. He had very little info, but soon my house was filled with friends, family, and several officers. We all started gathering by the door to carpool down to the hospital. As far as we knew he was only shot in the leg and we would be going to visit him. But as I grabbed my coat the chief pulled me back to the living room and sat me down on the couch. He told me Dan was gone, and I felt the most hideous emptiness inside. I sank down into the couch and then onto the floor. Dan's mom was rushed into another room because she started screaming. I can still hear her screams in my head to this day. We eventually all rode down to the hospital, and I was told I could see his body. I felt I had to, otherwise I would never truly believe that this had happened. After that it was all a blur: the funeral, the memorials, the trips to the capital, meeting the President, the governor, the cards and gifts. The loss was felt by so many more people than I could have ever imagined. Dan's personality was larger than life, and the amount of people he touched in his short 25 years was astounding. But it became clear that his death touched even more lives than he could have ever reached in life.

Dan and I had actually discussed how things would go if this did happen to him. He used to joke about how he would never live past 25 and that he wanted to be buried in the cemetery in Oceanside where all the original founders of the city were. He also told me I should remarry, and that is what allowed me to move on afterward, along with the fact that I had a son who needed a father and was still young enough not to remember the horrible event. It was also very clear how much I loved and depended on Dan. I have no regrets about our life together and the way things ended, except that I feel it was my pride that let him return to work that night and be put in the situation that ended his life.

Time passed, and through a mutual friend I met Jordan. We dated for several months and decided to get married shortly after that. Jordan is an amazing father to Wyatt and to our new son, Riggins. As horrible as Dan's death was, I know God brought great things out of it and I wouldn't change a thing. I know now that I wouldn't be who I am today without my life with Dan, and I'm so thankful for the years I had with Dan and the future I will have with Jordan.

- Katelyn

Earlier that summer, just before Katelyn's letter arrives, I walk through the scarred, burned-out landscape near Lake Tahoe after massive forest fires swept over the Angora ridge and decimated the area. A friend tells me that often the best thing possible for the forest is a fire, because the ashes enrich the soil and promote stronger renewal and growth. There are certain tree seeds that can only germinate from the heat of forest fires, and the seed cones can lie dormant for decades before sprouting any kind of growth. The forest needs the fire. It's the earth's way of feeding herself, and in time life emerges from the ashes.

Reading Katelyn's letter leaves me thinking that she has begun her own renewal, like a flower has somehow pushed up through the wreckage of Dan's death, so I start "From the Ashes" about the beauty that can grow from tragedy. I also wonder if somewhere God or Buddha or whoever is laughing at me as I ask my *Whys,* when the answers are everywhere around me in the lakes and rivers and oceans and mountains and deserts and ashes. Especially the ashes.

Autumn turns over before Sara comes over to help me finish "From the Ashes." She sings it a few days later downstairs while I play the song on a guitar that my friend Andy made for me. He has inlaid silhouettes of Kona and Stella, my new Labrador, on the back of the headstock, and I look at them as I play and remember that while Stella is now at my feet, just behind me tucked away on a shelf above the couch are Kona's ashes.

* * *

From the Ashes

i watched the pile burn
smoke across my sky
there are lessons to learn
in goodbye

i turned down this road
stripped of my disguise
as a new moon strode
across my eyes

from the ashes i watched
beauty rise

smoke faded away
and i began to hope
through this blanket of gray
green would grow

in time i found a friend
and to my surprise
the burn began to mend
before our eyes

from the ashes we watched
beauty rise

i watched the pile burn
smoke across my sky
there are lessons to learn
in goodbye

in the wreckage truth still lies
through the remnants of our lives
from the ashes we watch
beauty rise

*   *   *

These letters seem to bring out beautiful truths buried in the wreckage of tragedy. In Emily's letter, the beautiful truth in her loss is that she found love at all. For Kim, the beautiful truth in her pain growing up is that it gave her the capacity to help heal others later. And Alison has found the beautiful truth of the human spirit in Haiti's devastation.

I'm waiting on a wave when I realize that Katelyn's beautiful truth is in the moving on. She's fulfilling the promise she made to Dan when they talked about finishing what they've begun. She is raising a child and building a life in a loving environment, and that's what Dan would have wanted.

I talk to Jack about it, and he suggests we write a song about finishing what is begun. I think it's about Katelyn standing at the edge of that unfinished road she was on with Dan and Wyatt. But instead of turning around, she is building something new, right where the concrete and rebar of the old road holds hands with the new one. Right there at the edge.

*　　*　　*

Begun

my mom moved on when i was so young
i never did know my dad
but we had a house full of laughter and love
the best home a boy ever had

still growing up i wondered about him
til in a box under the bed
i found a letter he wrote to my mom
and held back the tears as i read it said

i love you more than life itself
but i know i'll probably die young
so when i'm gone i want you to go on
and finish what we have begun
oh finish what we have begun

i asked my mom what that letter meant
and why my dad went away
she said son there's a hero's call
and a job for those who stay

i love you more than life itself
but i know i'll probably die young
so when i'm gone i want you to go on
and finish what we have begun
oh finish what we have begun

there's no place to hide
this world ain't no free ride
you gotta take what's wrong
and try to make it right
that's why i'm here
far away from you dear
writing this letter tonight

now i ride under the same troubled sky
helping out like my old man did
i sit here and write with this pen in my hand
the same words to my wife and kid

i love you more than life itself
but i know i'll probably die young
so when i'm gone i want you to go on
and finish what we have begun

*   *   *

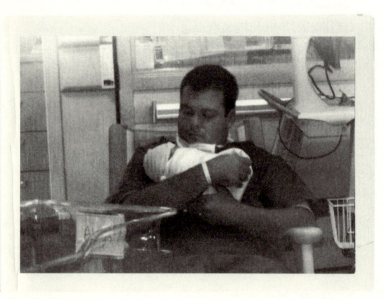

Dan and Wyatt

The Naysayers and I record "Begun" downstairs, with Jack singing the fatherly voice from the past in the choruses as an echoing reminder of service and its costs. Another voice from the past arrives a few days later in Nena Anderson, who has just sung with me on "Rescue" and is helping with harmonies on "Begun." When she sings, I close my eyes and I'm in an underground jazz club on West 3rd in 1935, taking shallow breaths to avoid the smoke hanging in the room. I open my eyes, hit the stop-recording button, and am back in my living room with the wind off the Pacific filtering through the half-open front door.

Nena wants to dive deeper into songwriting, which is why she reaches out a few months before when we meet at a local coffee shop. After hanging out a few times, we write "Hush" as a lullaby to Wyatt, something Katelyn might have sung to him in those late autumn hours when he wouldn't go to sleep. The hardest part of this song to write is the very last line, but out in the water one morning I realize that it may be way more difficult for Nena to sing, since she is a single mom.

We don't talk about it, but I wonder.

*   *   *

Hush

hush my darling
hush my dear
close your eyes your mama's here

hush my darling
should you weep
i will sing you off to sleep

if i could turn back time

hush my darling
hush my love
hear the angels up above

hush my darling
should you weep
i will pray your soul to keep

if i could turn back time

your papa would be coming home
your papa would be coming home
your papa would be coming home
tonight

hush my darling
hush my dear
close your eyes your mama's here

hush my darling
hush my love
hear the angels up above

if i could turn back time

your papa would be coming home
your papa would be coming home
but your papa he ain't coming home
tonight

*   *   *

We record "Hush" downstairs as a rock song to noisily reflect the turmoil Katelyn must have been going through in those early-morning hours when Wyatt wouldn't go to sleep. A few weeks later, we sing the song as a true lullaby for both her and Wyatt when we make a trip to Katelyn's house to play the songs for her. We surprise her under the guise of an interview, and the audio recorder on the table outside is left running while we introduce ourselves to Wyatt, by now a confident toddler.

Signs of the renewal and growth I was hoping for in "From the Ashes" are everywhere as Wyatt climbs up into Katelyn's lap and I get my guitar out. I start to play "Hush" into an air that is somehow heavy and light at the same time, as Wyatt hangs on to Katelyn's dress and listens to every word. I can barely look up at him, so I bury myself in my guitar as Nena sings, and continue to play along with Jack's "Begun" and Sara's "From the Ashes." Katelyn hides her feelings better than any of us do, but the air doesn't lie, and the sweet suffocation of honest emotion is everywhere around us.

I'm in the ocean early the next morning, thinking about how it seems fitting that I didn't sing any of the songs at Katelyn's house. This experience has been about other people's stories and songs, and that's what Katelyn's house was about, too: someone else singing someone else's story.

A local pod of dolphins comes over to play, and as I take off on a chest-high wave, I see a dorsal fin rise up next to me. The dolphin and I ride together, and I am so in the moment that I forget my thoughts, my body, and my self more completely than usual because I'm sharing the ride with an animal of such awesome grace. She dances under my board, switches direction, and glides just behind me as I forfeit turning and stand there, quietly in motion with her.

My mind takes over again as we both pull out of the wave. These moments are what my dreams are made of now, more so than all the things I thought I wanted *someday*. Surfing isn't about *someday*. It's about now. I let go of *someday* every time I take off on a wave and become more present in the moment. Life is better then, when I'm not thinking about me.

I paddle back out to the lineup wondering if the letting go I've been fighting hasn't been about letting go of dreams at all.

Maybe it was about letting go of me.

All these songs I've had a hand in, about someone else's story and rarely sung in my voice, and I'm happier than ever. It's my same dream of making a moment in someone's life better with a song, but it looks different now. I laugh as I realize that I call myself a songwriter, but I haven't written a song about myself in months.

And I take the next wave in, rush out of the water, up the stairs, and into the house, because my next thought overtakes me like the final sequence in a movie where all those scenes that didn't make sense before come together in a heartbeat.

Maybe I *was* somehow writing about myself.

Maybe my story has been there the whole time.

All this time, we had been one and the same.

— *Way of the Peaceful Warrior*

THE BOX

Dear Alex:

I wanted to share
with you. I am not a w...
...know how to articulate
...show how to...

...first Christmas as well as...

...None of them could... Remember when... you were talked... learned to... on the... for...

...you were... ...leaving for yo...

...k you for being here

I love you
Alex

On second thought, I balk at the idea. "This is kind of hippie-ish," I mutter as I move around the house with my wetsuit still on, pulling together the letters from Emily, Katelyn, Kim, and Alison and the songs we wrote for them. On top of the pile of letters and lyrics, I gather the napkins and notepads on which I've written scenes in my life as they passed by. I have so many notes scattered around the house from the last few years, in drawers and tour books and on my computer, that my wetsuit is almost dry by the time I find them all.

I read through some of these bar-napkin journals and find that many of the scenes in my own life loosely mirror the letters, and then I turn to the song lyrics.

My hopes, dreams, and fears are all there, deep water running still under the moving currents of the songs. There is my own hope for finding a partner underneath "My Love Will Find You," my own moment of pause before opening the door to my old house in "Love Began As a Whisper." There is my shivering dream as a naked child on a rocky beach in "Rescue," my imaginary coat of protection burning in "From the Ashes."

And at the bottom of the pile are the lyrics to "For the Sender." The last line is "Do you remember?" I do. I stand there in my kitchen, as the last traces of saltwater drip from my wetsuit onto the kitchen floor, and remember Kona.

I walk back to my bedroom, and as I'm changing into a pair of board shorts, I glance over at the corner where my collective bible of books lives. I turn through *The Grapes of Wrath,* until I find a page with the upper corner bent over, and read out loud: "Maybe all men got one big soul ever'body's a part of."

The idea doesn't sound quite as hippie-ish coming from Steinbeck, and I can imagine my story being part of a bigger one. I can see how the struggles and triumphs we talk about over dinner, or on the playground, or to the mirror, are unique because they come from different voices, but are all part of the same conversation. The stories belong to all of us.

So I read the letters again, and I see me.

I see my autumn in Emily's letter. Her loss remembered is mine, in the passing of my best friend.

I see my shelter in Kim's letter. Her story of addiction and homelessness is mine, in the drug-infected dream vacuum that used to be my safe place, but never will be again.

I see my search in Alison's letter. Her description of faith affirmed in the midst of human suffering is mine, in faith questioned as I watch my grandma disintegrate.

I see my well in Katelyn's letter. Her sudden emptying of sadness is mine, in the slow seeping suicide of Grace.

And as I play back the mental tape of visiting Katelyn and performing for her and Wyatt, I see the burned-out landscape of the Angora ridge. The beauty growing from the ashes is there, in little Wyatt.

As I'm stacking the letters back on top of the lyrics on my kitchen counter, I wonder how many other people out there have a letter tucked away in a dresser drawer or a box somewhere, a letter written but never sent.

Then I realize that I have my own.

I walk downstairs to the studio where a wooden box sits on a shelf above the couch. I open the lid, and my heart hurts when I see the plastic bag full of ashes with a rose draped over the top, along with a few strands of black hair and a paw print embedded in clay.

Next to the plastic bag there is a letter.

Dear Kona,

Thank you for being with me for so long. The times I was most alone, I was never really alone because you were always there. I am so sad you are leaving, but I know it's the right thing at the right time. I love you with everything I have and am so grateful this lasted as long as it did. I remember picking you up in Utah and you were so tiny and new. So much has happened since then. Oregon, then to Seattle, then to Manhattan Beach, then home to Leucadia. I'm happy that you spent time here in this house. You saw its first Christmas, as well as so many good times and good people. I am grateful for that.

All of those girlfriends. None of them could compete. You hated to be left alone. Remember when you clawed through the door when you were locked in the downstairs at 406? Or how you learned to open the bedroom window and climb out on the roof and would just be up there barking for me to come home? You never wanted to be alone, and I suppose I never did either, because I took you with me everywhere. I left you in the hotel room in Santa Barbara and you barked until you ended up in the manager's office. And all the Kona hair all over the place. You made a mark everywhere, and on everyone who knew you. There are a lot of people sad today because you are leaving. I suppose the one thing that never leaves is the pile of memories. But your leaving has made me feel like I am living deeper. Like maybe the shell around my heart has cracked a little, and I can actually feel something again. When I was in Boston, I didn't yet know you but had your name written down on a piece of paper along with a few other choices. You were kind of a beacon shining from the West, and when I left New England, I was leaving for you.

So much growing up for both of us. You were patient with all of my wandering and sometimes questionable decision making. I was patient with your frustration at being alone. We finally landed here in Leucadia, which has been your home for

*almost half of your life. A good 5 or 6 years. Maybe 4. Actually
5 years, almost to the day.*

*I will miss your smiling face when I come home. I will
miss your just being here. With me. You have been a part of me
for so long that I don't know what I was like before you. I suppose that's the closing of a chapter. Thank you for being here.*

I love you,

Alex

In the box with the letter and her
ashes is a torn piece of newspaper
from the week she died and a photo
taken the day after I got her, with her
head resting on the neck of my guitar
wedged between the seats.

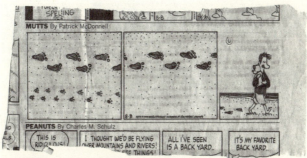

I am still carrying her.

I remember another photo, and I hunt around the house for it, through folders and albums and file cabinets before I find it at the bottom of a box marked PHOTOS: UNFRAMED.

We had stopped to get gas, and I bought a disposable camera. I was throwing away the plastic wrapping from the camera when I turned to see Kona's face resting on the side mirror, waiting for me to come back. It was one of the first pictures I ever took of her, and it was the same loyal, loving face I'd come back to for the next 14 years.

I fold the letter back up, tuck it back in the box with the photos, and close the lid.

I miss her.

CODA: *(music)*

concluding passage — It. L. cauda tail.

A few weeks after Kona died, Shawn Mullins came to San Diego to play a show, and I was asked to open for him. Shawn was a songwriting hero of mine when I was getting my feet (and everything else) wet in Seattle. He had a number one song on the radio at the time called "Lullaby," and I went to his concert by myself one rainy night at a theater downtown off Fifth Avenue. It gave me hope to see a guy with a guitar making a living with his own songs, especially in the Britney-Spears-infused world we were living in at the time. Walking to my truck after the show, I wondered whether there might someday be an audience out there for me, like there was for him. *Someday* is a word filled with hope and patience, that much I knew, and I was holding on to it tight. Our paths crossed here and there as the decade unfolded, but I never got to know Shawn until he came to San Diego that summer Kona died. I invited him and his tour manager to stay at my house after the concert, which I thought would be a change from the faceless hotels of the road.

The next morning after breakfast, I played Shawn a song
I had written called "The Table." He had recently lost his
dog, Roadie, who was much the same to him as Kona was to
me, and the song resonated with him after I told him the story
behind it.

"The Table" is about a man who has lost his partner to
cancer. I had no connection to the disease at the time and
wasn't sure why I was writing a song about it, but I didn't edit
the word *cancer* out of the first verse. Instead, I let the song
unfold and recorded it in my living room in early December,
with Kona and my new puppy Stella tangled up in the microphone cables and gnawing on drumsticks while we tracked.
A couple of days later I got the news that Kona was dying of
bone cancer and probably wouldn't make it to Christmas.

Kona was already dying of cancer when I wrote the song,
but I had no idea. She had been suffering in her quiet way for
a while, not complaining, just laying there at my feet night
after night. She was so stoic, so patient with pain, that it had
always been impossible to know when something was wrong.
When she was only a few years old, my dad and I took her on
a long hike through the Washington state wilderness. About
halfway through the hike, I noticed that it had been a few
minutes since she had caught up to us. She was always close
behind, so I traced my way back to find her silently laying on
her side, her paw pads ripped to shreds from a spine of shale
she had tried to cross only a few feet behind us.

She hadn't even whimpered as she walked over the mine-field of sharp stones, each step no doubt more excruciating than the one before. We carried her for a couple of miles until I could float her the rest of the way in the waist-deep water of a just-thawed alpine lake, every other step asking her why she didn't tell me she was hurt.

That was her way.

And that's probably why she didn't tell me she was sick, but one early December morning something didn't seem right so I took her to the vet. It wasn't until I was sitting under those white lights in the waiting room and heard the word *cancer* that I finally understood why I had written "The Table."

She lived longer than anyone anticipated and died in July of the following year, a few weeks before Shawn showed up in San Diego. After I told him the story, we went down to the beach so he could see where we surfed and where Kona had played every morning. He sat on the stairs above the sand and asked me if I'd like to open some more shows for him and maybe write a few songs with him, too. I couldn't believe what I was hearing. Touring and writing with Shawn had been a dream of mine for years, one of those dreams I was struggling to let go of that autumn after Kona died. I'd reached out to his management and booking agent over the years asking for the opportunity, but it wasn't until I'd finally let go of the pos-sibility that it appeared right there on the stairs in front of the house.

I flew to Atlanta early that December for a Christmas show with Shawn at the legendary Eddie's Attic. I started playing "The Table" at the end of my set, and when I sang the line "she's been gone about a year," I realized that it had been about a year since the night Kona was diagnosed. I sang the next lines of the first verse and heard her tail thumping against the floor as her friends said goodbye to her that Christmas, and I remembered carrying her to my bed and sitting on the edge, wondering what was next.

Two lines later in the song, Shawn and venue owner Eddie came up on stage next to me. They had rehearsed the song outside in the cold Georgia night beforehand and came in on the first chorus as if we'd been singing "The Table" together for years.

In those moments onstage I felt something come full circle. I was singing about the loss of my closest friend and the letting go of old dreams, while one of those dreams I thought had died with her was standing to my left, behind a microphone, singing. With me. Shawn and Eddie followed along as I went into an impromptu "Silent Night." After the line "Sleep in heavenly peace," I silently told Kona I hoped she was sleeping peacefully somewhere, too; I missed her; and Merry Christmas. I thanked the crowd and walked off the stage wondering how many more moments like this I would ever have. I tried to hold the moment for as long as I could, and when I couldn't hold it anymore I did my best to let it go into the suburban Atlanta night, hoping that someday a space in time like this would come back to me again.

Someone recorded that show and gave me a CD of the performance, and while the CD kind of skips here and there and my playing is shaky, hearing Shawn find his way to the first chorus runs deep in me every time I hear it. That moment will always remind me of the importance of being patient and allowing everything to unfold in its own time. It will always remind me to trust the process.

And I will always be grateful for that moment.

*   *   *

The Table

he sits down at the table
she's been gone about a year
he says the cancer took her sudden
but her spirit keeps her near
right here

he says the world keeps on turning
like it don't know that she's gone
so i hold on to moments
and i turn the radio on

we dance around the room
like we used to do and then
she's in my arms again
boy i'm telling you
we dance around the room
and then the music ends

then i go back to being me
and i turn down the lights

sometimes i stare at the ceiling
sometimes i close my eyes

we dance around the room
like we used to do and then
she's in my arms again
boy i'm telling you
we dance around the room
and then the music ends

every time i try to sleep
every time i think she's next me
every time she makes me believe

he gets up from the table
says if heaven's up to me
she's gonna meet me down at the old house
and slowly

we'll dance around the room
like we used to do and then
she's in my arms again
boy i'm telling you
we'll dance around that room
and the music will never end

*　　*　　*

I can barely make out the blurred image of myself holding Stella as a puppy in my favorite photo of Kona. Kona's muzzle is gray, and her eyes are trained up and away, as if she is looking into a future she knows is coming but I can't quite see yet. The cancer is already in her, already spreading, and she is already at peace.

I tell people I wrote "The Table" for Kona.

But, like that letter to her still tucked away in a wooden box above the couch, it was more for the sender.

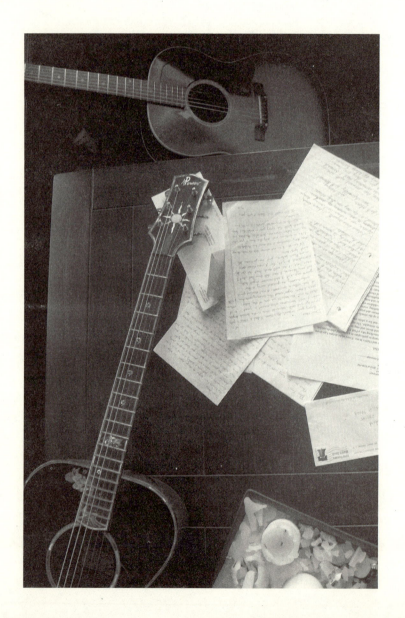

Thanks to my friends for their talent and time. And to Kona for being there.

Sean Watkins

Sara Watkins

Jon Foreman

Jordan Pundik

Nena Anderson

Molly Jenson

Jack Tempchin

Melissa Grove

Ryan Hilbert

Alex Gorosh

Jeff Wiant

Stefanie Bond

Colin Whyte

Rick DeVoe

Kristen Foster

Erin Hawk

David Thoener

Deane Cote

Isaac Marr

Patrick McClory

Dan Bailey

Rami Jaffee

Brian Young

Andy Powers

Keith Tutt

Shawn Mullins

Kip Conner

Andrew Jandt

And Emily, Kim, Alison, and Katelyn.

For the Sender *

Written by Alex Woodard and Sean Watkins
Published by Woodshack Music (ASCAP) / Perfect Left (ASCAP)

My Love Will Find You

Written by Alex Woodard
Published by Woodshack Music (ASCAP)

Never Alone

Written by Alex Woodard and Jon Foreman
Published by Woodshack Music (ASCAP) / Rubadub Rublishing Publishing (ASCAP)

Unbroken †

Written by Jon Foreman
Published by Rubadub Rublishing Publishing (ASCAP)

Love Began As a Whisper

Written by Alex Woodard
Published by Woodshack Music (ASCAP)

The Right Words

Written by Alex Woodard
Published by Woodshack Music (ASCAP)

Rescue

Written by Alex Woodard
Published by Woodshack Music (ASCAP)

Act of God

Written by Alex Woodard and Jack Tempchin
Published by Woodshack Music (ASCAP) / Night River Publishing (ASCAP)

Broken Wide Open

Written by Alex Woodard, Sara Watkins, and Jack Tempchin
Published by Woodshack Music (ASCAP) / Fiddle and Fall (ASCAP) / Night River Publishing (ASCAP)

From the Ashes

Written by Alex Woodard and Sara Watkins
Published by Woodshack Music (ASCAP) / Fiddle and Fall (ASCAP)

Begun

Written by Alex Woodard and Jack Tempchin
Published by Woodshack Music (ASCAP) / Night River Publishing (ASCAP)

Hush
Written by Alex Woodard and Nena Anderson
Published by Woodshack Music (ASCAP) / Antique Rodeo (BMI)

The Table Live at Eddie's Attic
Written by Alex Woodard
Engineered by Kip Conner
Published by Woodshack Music (ASCAP)

All songs ℗ 2012 For the Sender LLC

Produced by Alex Woodard
     except * by Sean Watkins and † with Jon Foreman
Mixed by David Thoener
Mastered by Glenn Meadows/Mayfield Mastering
Book Design by Nena Anderson/Dungbeetle Creative

Jon Foreman appears courtesy of Atlantic Records
Jordan Pundik appears courtesy of Epitaph Records
Sara Watkins appears courtesy of Nonesuch Records
Shawn Mullins appears courtesy of Vanguard Records

Please visit us at **www.ForTheSender.com** to learn about
the charitable causes chosen by the senders, including Kim's shelter
and Alison's clinic.

ABOUT THE AUTHOR

When he's not surfing in a little beach town north of San Diego, Alex lives with a big dog and a bigger horse in the mountains of Idaho.

For further info, visit: **www.ForTheSender.com** or **www.AlexWoodard.com**.

If you'd like to have your own **handwritten**
letter considered for a song by Alex and the
For the Sender musicians, please mail it to:

For the Sender
c/o Hay House
P.O. Box 5100
Carlsbad, CA 92018

While a song can't be written about every letter,
we do read them all. Please be sure to include your contact
information so that we can reach you if we need to.
Thank you.

We hope you enjoyed this Hay House book. If you'd like
to receive our online catalog featuring additional information
on Hay House books and products, or if you'd like to find out
more about the Hay Foundation, please contact:

Hay House, Inc., P.O. Box 5100, Carlsbad, CA 92018-5100
(760) 431-7695 or (800) 654-5126
(760) 431-6948 (fax) or (800) 650-5115 (fax)
www.hayhouse.com® • **www.hayfoundation.org**

*   *   *

Published and distributed in Australia by: Hay House Australia Pty. Ltd.,
18/36 Ralph St., Alexandria NSW 2015 • *Phone:* 612-9669-4299
Fax: 612-9669-4144 • www.hayhouse.com.au

Published and distributed in the United Kingdom by:
Hay House UK, Ltd., 292B Kensal Rd., London W10 5BE • *Phone:*
44-20-8962-1230 • *Fax:* 44-20-8962-1239 • www.hayhouse.co.uk

Published and distributed in the Republic of South Africa by:
Hay House SA (Pty), Ltd., P.O. Box 990, Witkoppen 2068
Phone/Fax: 27-11-467-8904 • www.hayhouse.co.za

Published in India by: Hay House Publishers India,
Muskaan Complex, Plot No. 3, B-2, Vasant Kunj, New Delhi 110 070
Phone: 91-11-4176-1620 • *Fax:* 91-11-4176-1630 • www.hayhouse.co.in

Distributed in Canada by: Raincoast, 9050 Shaughnessy St.,
Vancouver, B.C. V6P 6E5 • *Phone:* (604) 323-7100
Fax: (604) 323-2600 • www.raincoast.com

*   *   *

Take Your Soul on a Vacation

Visit **www.HealYourLife.com**® to regroup, recharge,
and reconnect with your own magnificence.
Featuring blogs, mind-body-spirit news, and
life-changing wisdom from Louise Hay and friends.

Visit **www.HealYourLife.com** today.

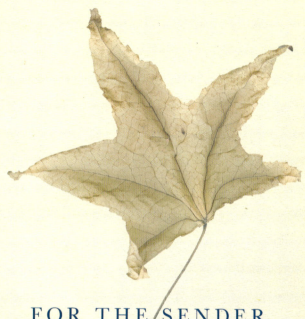

FOR THE SENDER

Four Letters. Twelve Songs. One Story.

Dear Alex:

If you'd like to stay informed about *For the Sender* news, including events and products, please visit **www.ForTheSender.com** or **www.HayHouse.com**. Follow Alex Woodard and Hay House on Facebook and Twitter.

Sometimes a letter is like a prayer; it's more for the sender than the receiver.

Now it's your turn to write a few words to someone else; you might find that it does you both some good.

Front photo: Alden DeSoto

Inspired by the book FOR THE SENDER by Alex Woodard (Hay House), **www.ForTheSender.com**. Available everywhere books are sold, or save 20% at **www.HayHouse.com**.